푸른 빛의 소녀가

The Blue Light Girl

일러두기

책에 담긴 그림은 우크라이나 태생의 러시아 화가 카지미르 세베리노비치 말레비치(Kazimir Severinovich Malevich, 1879-1935)의 작품을 바탕으로 재구성한 것입니다.

Note The paintings in this book, *The Blue Light Girl*, are reconstructions based on the work of Ukrainian-born Russian painter Kazimir Severinovich Malevich(1879-1935).

THE BLUE LIGHT GIRL

박노해 시 그림책
Park Nohae's
Poetry Picture Book

지구별의 아이들에게

To Planet Earth's Children

저 먼 행성에서 불시착한
푸른 빛의 소녀가 내게 물었다

**Crash-landing from a distant planet,
the Blue Light Girl asked me:**

지구에서 좋은 게 뭐죠?

What is good on Earth?

꽃과 나무요
기품 있는 여인과 아이들요
저 푸른 산능선과 강물과 들녘의 가을요

Flowers and trees.
Graceful women and children.
Those blue mountain ridges, rivers, autumn fields.

시와 예술과 감동이요
가슴 떨리는 생의 신비와 경이로움요

**Poetry, art and emotion.
The mystery and wonder of thrilling life.**

선과 정의가 승리하는 거요

Goodness and justice victorious.

사랑,
죽음보다 강한 사랑의 힘요

Love,
the power of love stronger than death.

그럼 지구에서 슬픈 게 뭐죠?

So what is sad on Earth?

중력의 무거움요
인생의 짧음이요
너무 자주 아픈 몸과 번뇌로 가득한 마음요

The burden of gravity.
The brevity of life.
The body so often sick, the heart so full of anguish.

지구를 짓누르고 있는 폐기물과 무기들요

The waste and weapons burdening the Earth.

지구를 벗어나지도
나를 벗어나지도 못하는 거요

**I cannot escape from the Earth
or from myself.**

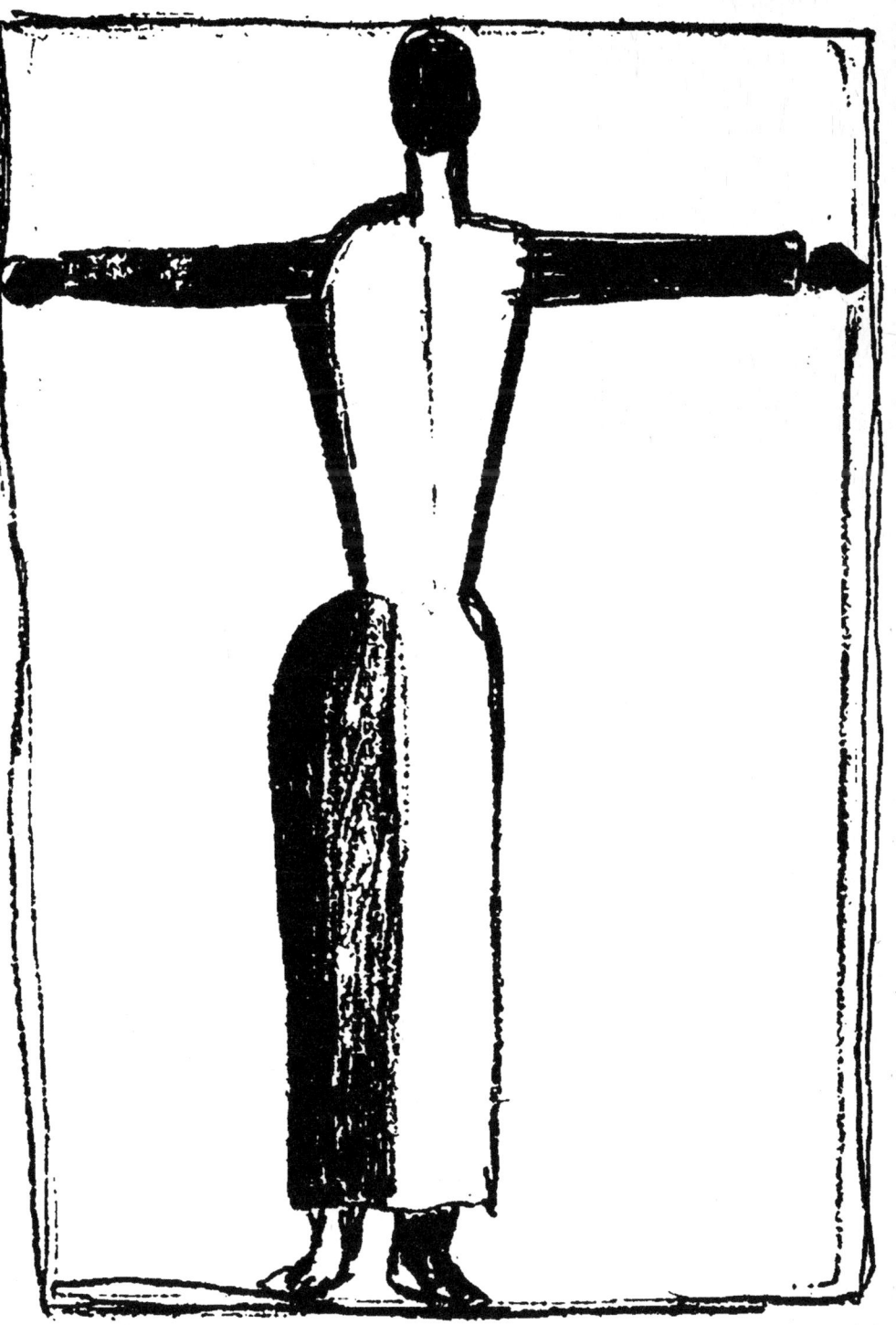

소유하고 인정받는 데 짧은 생을 다 쓰느라
자기 자신마저 알지 못한 채 떠나가는 거요

**After spending a short life in pursuit of possession and recognition
leaving without ever knowing oneself.**

지금 나랑 같이 다른 행성으로 갈래요?
소녀가 둥근 빛으로 내게 손을 내밀었다

Would you like to go to another planet with me now?
The girl held out a hand to me in a round light.

음… 아니요
여기가 나의 지옥 나의 천국이에요

Well… no.
Here is my hell, my heaven.

여기 지구엔 온 우주에서
내가 제일 사랑하는 사람들과
나의 친구들이 살고 있거든요

The people and my friends
whom I love the most in the universe
are living here on Earth.

**난 내게 전승되고 간직해온 이 사랑의 불을
지구별의 아이들에게 꼭 전해주어야 해요**

I have to pass on this fire of love,
handed down to me and treasured,
to Planet Earth's children.

그럼 당신의 기도는 뭐죠?

Then what is your prayer?

난 우주의 개미 한 마리, 한 점 먼지 정도겠죠
하지만 나는 영혼을 가진 인간이고
온 우주를 품고 있는 간절한 한 송이 꽃이죠

Maybe I'm merely an ant in the universe, a grain of dust.
But I am a human being with a soul,
I am an ardent flower embracing the whole universe.

이 무력한 사랑의 길에서
많이 상처받고 고독하고 슬프지만
그래도 어쩔 수 없어요   난

On this path of powerless love
I'm deeply wounded, lonely and sad
but I can't help it.

주지 않는 사랑은 지고 나르는 고통이니까요

Because the love that you withhold is the pain

hat you carry.

내 생의 기도는 단 하나,

There is only one prayer in my life:

땅에서와같이 하늘에서도
삶에서와같이 영혼에서도
나에서와같이 세상에서도

As on earth, so too in heaven.
As in life, so too in the soul.
As in me, so too in the world.

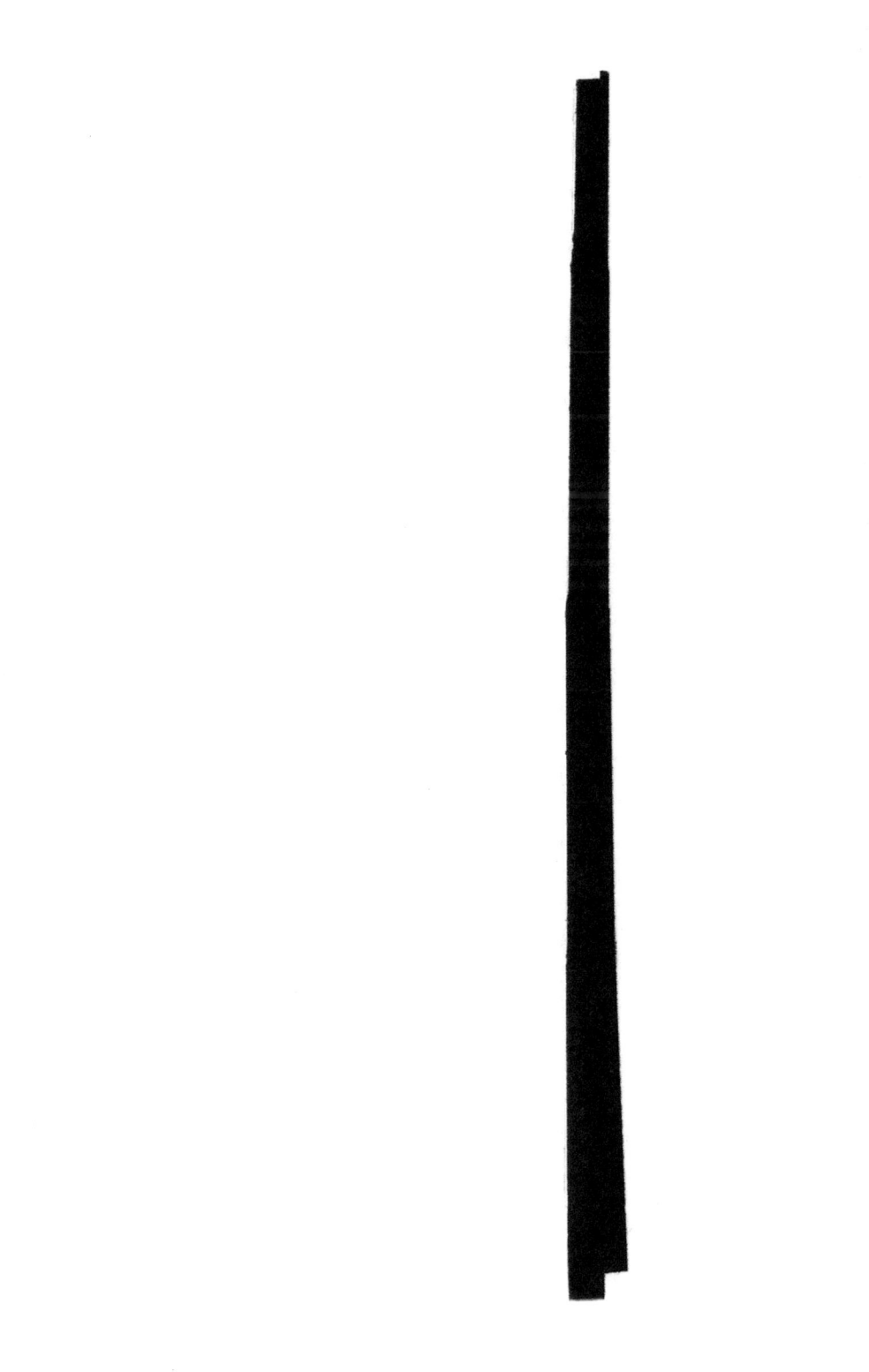

소녀가 빛으로 사라지며 내게 속삭였다

당신에겐 중력도 은총이군요
사랑한 기억으로 영원을 사는군요

As the girl disappeared into light she whispered to me:

Even gravity is grace for you.
You live forever with memories of love.

안녕, 우린 다시 만날 거예요

Farewell, we will meet again.

박노해 시인
Poet Park Nohae

지은이
박 노 해

1957 전라남도에서 태어났다. 16세에 상경해 낮에는 노동자로 일하고 밤에는 선린상고(야간)를 다녔다. **1984** 스물일곱 살에 첫 시집 『노동의 새벽』을 출간했다. 이 시집은 군사독재 정권의 금서 조치에도 100만 부 가까이 발간되며 한국 사회와 문단을 충격으로 뒤흔들었다. 감시를 피해 사용한 박노해라는 필명은 '박해받는 노동자 해방'이라는 뜻으로, 이때부터 '얼굴 없는 시인'으로 알려졌다. **1989** 〈남한사회주의노동자동맹〉(사노맹)을 결성했다. **1991** 7년여의 수배생활 끝에 안기부에 체포, 24일간의 고문 후 '반국가단체 수괴' 죄목으로 사형이 구형되고 무기징역에 처해졌다. **1993** 감옥 독방에서 두 번째 시집 『참된 시작』을 출간했다. **1997** 옥중에세이 『사람만이 희망이다』를 출간했다. **1998** 7년 6개월의 수감 끝에 석방되었다. 이후 민주화운동 유공자로 복권됐으나 국가보상금을 거부했다. **2000** "과거를 팔아 오늘을 살지 않겠다"며 권력의 길을 뒤로 하고 비영리 사회운동단체 〈나눔문화〉(www.nanum.com)를 설립했다. **2003** 이라크 전쟁터에 뛰어들면서, 전 세계 가난과 분쟁 현장에서 평화활동을 이어왔다. **2010** 낡은 흑백 필름 카메라로 기록해온 사진을 모아 첫 사진전 「라 광야」展과 「나 거기에 그들처럼」展(세종문화회관)을 열었다. 304편의 시를 엮어 12년 만의 시집 『그러니 그대 사라지지 말아라』를 출간했다. **2012** 나눔문화가 운영하는 〈라 카페 갤러리〉에서 박노해 사진전을 상설 개최하고 있다. 현재까지 18번째 전시를 이어가고 있으며, 총 30만 명의 관람객이 다녀갔다. **2014** 아시아 사진전 「다른 길」展(세종문화회관) 개최와 함께 사진에세이 『다른 길』을 출간했다. **2019** 박노해 사진에세이 시리즈 『하루』, 『단순하게 단단하게 단아하게』, 『길』을 출간했다. **2020** 감옥에서부터 30년 동안 써온 단 한 권의 책, '우주에서의 인간의 길'을 담은 사상서를 집필 중이다. '적은 소유로 기품 있게' 살아가는 삶의 공동체 〈참사람의 숲〉을 꿈꾸며, 오늘도 시인의 작은 정원에서 꽃과 나무를 심고 기르며 새로운 혁명의 길로 나아가고 있다.

매일 아침, 사진과 글로 시작하는 하루 「박노해의 걷는 독서」 parknohae park_nohae

Writer
Park Nohae

Park Nohae is a legendary poet, photographer and revolutionary. He was born in 1957. While working as a laborer in his 20s, he began to reflect and write poems on the sufferings of the laboring class. He then took the pseudonym Park Nohae ("No" means "laborers," "Hae" means "liberation"). At the age of twenty-seven, Park published his first collection of poems, titled *The Dawn of Labor*, in 1984. Despite official bans, this collection sold nearly a million copies, and it shook Korean society with its shocking emotional power. Since then, he became an intensely symbolic figure of resistance, often called the "Faceless Poet." For several years the government authorities tried to arrest him in vain. He was finally arrested in 1991. After twenty-four days of investigation, with illegal torture, the death penalty was demanded for his radical ideology. He was finally sentenced to life imprisonment. After seven and a half years in prison, he was pardoned in 1998. Thereafter, he was reinstated as a contributor to the democratization movement, but he refused any state compensation. Park decided to leave the way for power, saying, "I will not live today by selling the past," and he established a nonprofit social movement organization "Nanum Munhwa," meaning "Culture of Sharing," (www.nanum.com) faced with the great challenges confronting global humanity. In 2003, right after the United States' invasion of Iraq, he flew to the field of war. Since then, he often visits countries that are suffering from war and poverty, such as Iraq, Palestine, Pakistan, Sudan, Tibet and Banda Aceh, in order to raise awareness about the situation through his photos and writings. He continues to hold photo exhibitions, and a total of 300,000 visitors have so far visited his exhibitions. He is writing a book of reflexions, the only such book he has written during the thirty years since prison, "The Human Path in Space." Dreaming of the Forest of True People, a life-community living "a graceful life with few possessions," the poet is still planting and growing flowers and trees in his small garden, advancing along the path toward a new revolution.

Every morning poem & photo, 「Park Nohae's Reading while Walking」 parknohae park_nohae

박노해 저서   Books by Park Nohae

길 박노해 사진에세이 03

박노해 시인이 20여 년 동안 기록해온 유랑노트, 「박노해 사진에세이」시리즈. 그 세 번째 책『길』에는 '인간의 길, 시대의 길'에 대한 통찰이 담긴 서문과 14개 나라에서 기록한 37점의 흑백사진이 유장하게 펼쳐지며, 길 찾는 우리에게 뜨거운 용기를 전한다. "길을 잃으면 길이 찾아온다. 길을 걸으면 길이 시작된다. 길은 걷는 자의 것이니." (박노해)

136p | 18,000KRW | 2020

The Path Park Nohae Photo Essay 03

Poet Park Nohae's notes from his past twenty years of wandering. In the series "Park Nohae Photo Essay," the third volume, *The Path*, contains a preface with insights on "the human path, the age's path," and a magnificent spread of thirty-seven black and white photographs taken in fourteen countries, offering us heart-warming courage as we seek for a path. "If you lose your way, the path will find you. If you start to walk, the path will begin. The path belongs to the walker." (Park Nohae)

노동의 새벽

1984년, 27살의 '얼굴 없는 시인'이 쓴 시집 한 권이 세상을 뒤흔들었다. 독재정부의 금서 조치에도 100만 부 이상 발간되며 화인처럼 새겨진 불멸의 고전. 억압받는 천만 노동자의 영혼의 북소리로 울려퍼진 노래. "박노해는 역사이고 상징이며 신화다. 문학사적으로나 사회사적으로 우리는 그런 존재를 다시 만날 수 없을지 모른다." (문학평론가 도정일)

172p | 12,000KRW | 2014
30th Anniversary Edition

The Dawn of Labor

In 1984, an anthology of poems written by twenty-seven years old "faceless poet" shook Korean society. Recorded as a million seller despite the publication ban under military dictatorship, it became an immortal classic ingrained like a marking iron. It was a song echoing down with the throbbing pulses of ten million workers' souls. "Park Nohae is a history, a symbol, and a myth. All the way through the history of literature and society alike, we may never meet such a being again." (Doh Jeong-il, literary critic)

사람만이 희망이다

서른 네 살의 나이에 '불온한 혁명가'로 무기징역을 선고 받은 박노해. 그가 1평 남짓한 감옥 독방에 갇혀 7년여 동안 써내려간 옥중에세이. "90년대 최고의 정신적 각성"으로 기록되는 이 책은, 희망이 보이지 않는 오늘날 더 큰 울림으로 되살아난다. 살아있는 한 희망은 끝나지 않았다고. 다시, 사람만이 희망이라고.

320p | 15,000KRW | 2015

Only a Person is Hope

Park Nohae was sentenced to life imprisonment as a "rebellious revolutionary" when he was thirty-four years old. This essay written in solitary confinement measuring about three sq. m. for seven years. This book is recorded as the "best spiritual awakening in the 90s," is born again with the bigger impression today when there seems to be no hope at all. As long as you live, hope never ends. Again, only a person is hope.

그러니 그대 사라지지 말아라

영혼을 뒤흔드는 시의 정수. 저항과 영성, 교육과 살림, 아름다움과 혁명 그리고 사랑까지 붉디 붉은 304편의 시가 담겼다. 인생의 갈림길에서 길을 잃고 헤매는 순간마다 어디를 펼쳐 읽어도 좋을 책. 입소문만으로 이 시집을 구입한 6만 명의 독자가 증명하는 감동. "그러니 그대 사라지지 말아라" 그 한 마디가 나를 다시 살게 한다.

560p | 18,000KRW | 2010

So You Must Not Disappear

The essence of soul-shaking poetry! This anthology of 304 poems as red as its book cover, narrating resistance, spirituality, education, living, the beautiful, revolution and love. Whenever you're lost at a crossroads of your life, it will guide you with any page of it moving you. The intensity of moving is evidenced by the 60,000 readers who have bought this book only through word-of-mouth. "So you must not disappear." This one phrase makes me live again.

다른 길

"우리 인생에는 각자가 진짜로 원하는 무언가가 있다. 나에게는 분명, 나만의 다른 길이 있다."(박노해) 인디아에서 파키스탄, 라오스, 버마, 인도네시아, 티베트까지 지도에도 없는 마을로 떠나는 여행. 그리고 그 길의 끝에서 진정한 나를 만나는 새로운 여행에세이. '이야기가 있는 사진'이 한 걸음 다른 길로, 좋은 삶으로 우리를 안내한다.

352p | 19,500KRW | 2014

Another Way

"In our lives, there is something which each of us really wants. For me, certainly, I have my own way, different from others" (Park Nohae). From India, Pakistan, Laos, Burma, Indonesia to Tibet, a journey to villages nowhere to be seen on the map. And a new essay of meeting true self at the end of the road. "Image with a story" guide us to another way, a step to good life.

나 거기에 그들처럼

인류의 가장 아픈 땅에서 낡은 흑백 필름 카메라와 오래된 만년필을 들고 현장의 진실을 기록해온 박노해. 그의 첫 사진집이자 아프리카, 중동, 아시아, 중남미 10여년의 작품을 총망라한 대작. "아는 만큼 보이는 것이 아니다. 사랑한 만큼 보이는 것이다."(박노해) 135컷의 '빛으로 쓴 시詩'가 가슴 깊이 울려온다.

300p | 100,000KRW | 2018
Revised Edition

Like Them, I am There

Park Nohae has been reported by an old film camera and fountain pen in most painful areas on the Earth. This book is his first photographic collection and a masterpiece bringing together photos taken in Africa, the Middle East, Asia, Central and South America over the course of ten years. "We don't see as much as we know; we see as much as we love."(Park Nohae) This "Poem written with light" of 135 works ring so profoundly to the heart.

박노해 시 그림책
푸른 빛의 소녀가

초판 8쇄 발행 2021년 3월 11일
초판 1쇄 발행 2020년 11월 3일

지은이 박노해

그림 카지미르 말레비치　디자인 홍동원
번역 안선재　편집 김예슬　제작 윤지혜
5도 분판 아트프린팅 유화컴퍼니　홍보 이상훈
종이 월드페이퍼　인쇄 경북프린팅
제본 광성문화사　후가공 이지앤비

발행인 임소희　발행처 느린걸음
출판등록 2002.3.15 제300-2009-109호
주소 서울시 종로구 사직로8길 34, 330호
전화 02-733-3773　팩스 02-734-1976
이메일 slow-walk@slow-walk.com
홈페이지 www.slow-walk.com

ⓒ 박노해 2020
ISBN 978-89-91418-30-1 03810

Park Nohae's Poetry Picture Book
The Blue Light Girl

First edition, 8th publishing, Mar. 11, 2021
First edition, first publishing, Nov. 3, 2020

Written by Park Nohae

Painting by Kazimir Severinovich Malevich
Designed by Hong Dongwon
Translation by Brother Anthony of Taizé
Edited by Kim Yeseul　Print Making by Yun Jihye
5Color Separation&Artprinting by UHWACOMPANY
Marketing by Lee Sanghoon

Publisher Im Sohee
Publishing Company Slow Walking
Address Rm330, 34, Sajik-ro 8-gil,
Jongno-gu, Seoul, Republic of Korea
Tel 82-2-7333773　Fax 82-2-7341976
E-mail slow-walk@slow-walk.com
Website www.slow-walk.com

ⓒ Park Nohae 2020
ISBN 978-89-91418-30-1 03810

우리 모두는
 별에서 온 아이들

네 안에는

 별이 빛나고 있어

We are all children come from the stars.

A star is shining within you.

박노해 Park Nohae